PLAY YOUR GUITAR
IN
2 WEEKS

Joseph Parker

GW00419862

foulsham
LONDON · NEW YORK · TORONTO · SYDNEY

foulsham
Yeovil Road, Slough, Berkshire SL1 4JH

ISBN 0-572-01610-7

Copyright © 1991 and 1966. Editors and Engineers Ltd.

All rights reserved.

The Copyright Act (1956) prohibits (subject to
certain very limited exceptions) the making of
copies of any copyright work or of a substantial
part of such a work, including the making of
copies by photocopying or similar process.
Written permission to make a copy or copies
must therefore normally be obtained from the
publisher in advance. It is advisable to consult
the publisher if in any doubt as to the legality of
any copying which is to be undertaken.

Printed in England by St Edmundsbury Press Ltd,
Bury St Edmunds, Suffolk

CONTENTS

PRACTICE SONGS

INTRODUCTION

Today the guitar is enjoying an unprecedented popularity. Guitars are predominant instruments in folk-singing groups, "go-go" or rock-and-roll combos, and country-and-western bands. The guitar has always been included in jazz groups and dance orchestras also.

Anyone who has two hands and the normal complement of fingers can learn to play the guitar. The only additional requirement is having the necessary perseverance to thoroughly master the lessons in this book.

The guitar is used mainly to accompany singers or other instruments, such as violins or various types of wind instruments; therefore, in order to use the guitar for accompaniment, it is only necessary to learn certain combinations of chords. This book is designed to thoroughly instruct the aspiring guitarist in the mastery of all the chords necessary to become a first rate accompanist.

CHOOSING A GUITAR

The primary consideration in choosing a guitar is simply to find the guitar that is most comfortable for you.

Guitar Sizes

Guitars come in many shapes and sizes. Generally a small person will be more comfortable with a small guitar, while a large person will find a larger model more to his liking.

Neck Sizes

The width of the neck is also very important. A person with small hands should choose a guitar with a narrow neck while a person with large hands should choose a guitar with a wider neck.

The simple tests to follow are:

1. Place the ball of the left thumb in the center of the back of the neck and make sure that all four fingers can reach all six strings without strain. If the guitar does not meet this test, the neck is too wide for you.
2. Depress each string with each finger, making sure that each finger can depress each string without touching the adjacent strings. If the guitar does not meet this test, the neck is too narrow for you.

JUDGING BY THE 12TH FRET

The next consideration for choosing a guitar is to make sure the strings fret true. To do this, pluck each string in the "open," or unfretted, position; then depress each string at the 12th fret and pluck it again. The second sound should be exactly one octave higher than the first. If the second sound is sharp or flat in relation to the first sound, the guitar is, in effect, out of tune with itself.

This condition is usually caused by the neck being warped. If this is the case, the author strongly recommends considering a different instrument. This condition can also be caused by the bridge being out of position. This can sometimes be cured by moving the bridge closer or more distant from the end of the finger board or by raising or lowering the bridge.

CHOOSING A GUITAR

Guitar Types

Country-and-western or folk-singing guitar.

This type guitar is characterized by a flat back and top and a large, round sound hole. These guitars have a very strong full sound. They are not adaptable to electronic amplification.

Rock-and-roll guitar.

This type guitar is characterized by having a solid wood block instead of an acoustic sound chamber. These guitars work only with electronic amplifiers and are completely silent when played without electronic amplification.

Orchestral or jazz guitar.

This type guitar is characterized by having an arched back and front and violin type *f* sound holes. These guitars are playable both with and without electronic amplification. They can be purchased with or without contact microphones attached. The guitars that do not have contact microphones attached can be converted easily by purchasing a contact microphone from any music dealer and attaching it yourself.

9

HOW TO HOLD AND FINGER THE GUITAR

Holding the Guitar

Seated position.

Standing position
with strap.

Straps with instructions for attaching are available at any
music store.

HOLDING THE PICK

This is the pick.

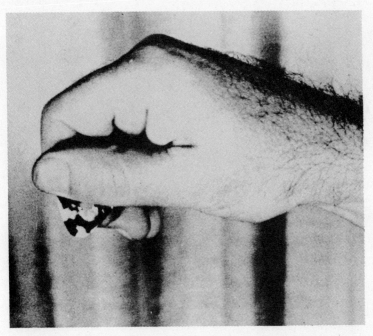

Hold pick firmly between thumb and index finger of right hand.

POSITION OF LEFT HAND

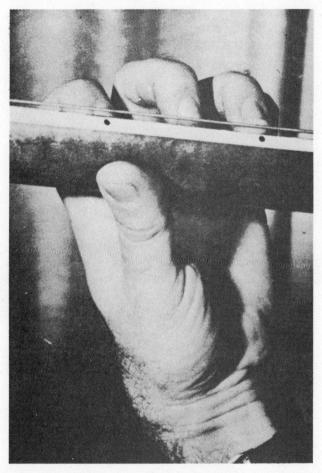

Correct position for left hand.

Ball of thumb should be in center of neck on the thickest part. Keep palm of left hand away from the neck.

POSITION OF RIGHT HAND

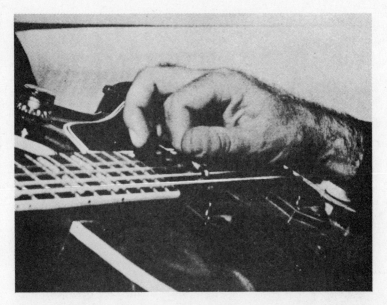

Correct position of right hand.

FINGERING AND TUNING

Fingering Schematic

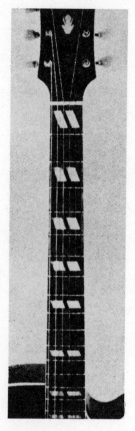

The fingerboard.

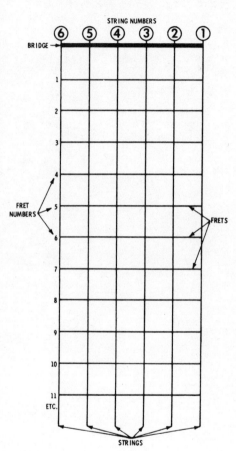

TUNING WITH PIANO

The six strings should be tuned to the same pitch as the six piano notes shown below:

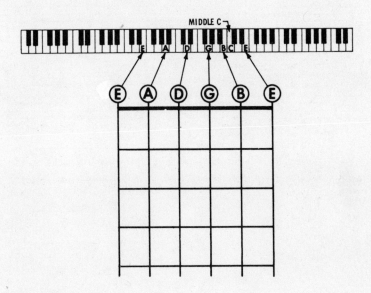

TUNING WITH PITCH PIPE

PIANO NOTATION
(CONCERT PITCH)

STRING GUITAR NOTATION
(ONE OCTAVE HIGHER)

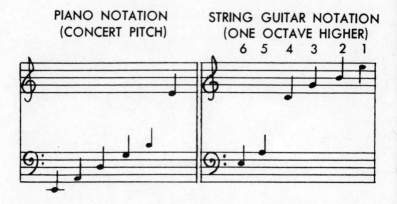

If a piano is unavailable, pitch pipes with instructions for use in tuning a guitar are available from any music store.

FINGERING AND TUNING

Chain Tuning—A Third Method of Tuning

1. Tune the sixth string to the same pitch as the E or twelfth key to the left of middle C on the piano.

2. Place finger behind the fifth fret on the 6th string. This will give you the pitch for the 5th string (A).

3. Place finger behind the fifth fret on the 5th string. This will give you the pitch for the 4th string (D).

4. Place finger behind the fifth fret on the 4th string. This will give you the pitch for the 3rd string (G).

5. Place finger behind the *fourth* fret on the 3rd string. This will give you the pitch for the 2nd string (B).

6. Place finger behind the fifth fret on the 2nd string. This will give you the pitch for the 1st string (E).

STRUMMING TO TIME SIGNATURE

Striking the Strings

The object in strumming the guitar is to strike the bass note with the pick, followed by strumming the rest of the strings indicated, then striking the alternate bass note with the pick, followed by strumming the same strings as before.

The following symbols will be used throughout the balance of this book:

    = Bass note.

    = Alternate bass note.

/ / / = Strokes of pick over strings.

    = Rest (do not play).

TIME SIGNATURE EXPLAINED

$\frac{4}{4}$ or C = Common time.

PLAY CHORDS IN THIS MANNER:

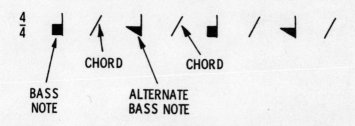

$\frac{3}{4}$ = Waltz time.

PLAY CHORDS IN THIS MANNER:

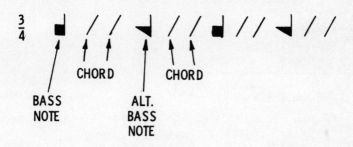

The C Chord

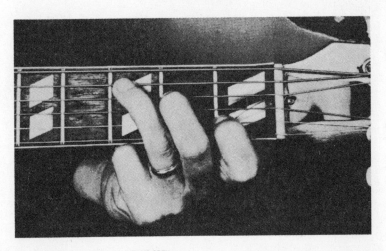

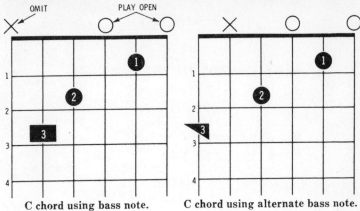

C chord using bass note.   C chord using alternate bass note.

Practice this chord until tone is clear. When you have mastered this, practice playing several times and

The G⁷ Chord

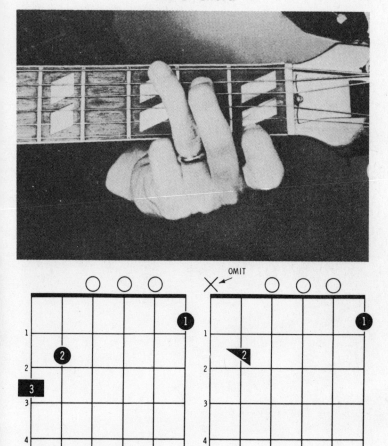

G⁷ chord using bass note.   G⁷ chord using alternate bass note.

Practice this chord in the same manner as the C chord.

Practice

Now that you have mastered the C and G^7 chords, practice playing the two chords as outlined below.

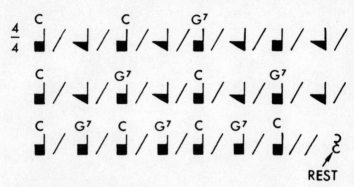

(rest) means do not play.

OUR FIRST SONG

— SKIP TO MY LOU —

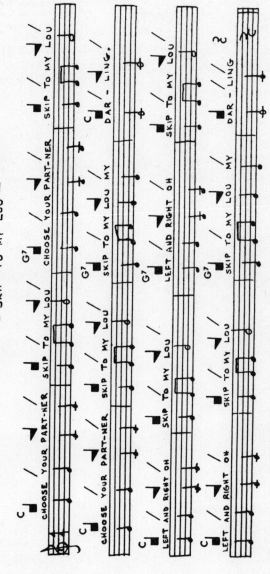

— NOTE — CONTINUE PLAYING THE C CHORD UNTIL YOU REACH THE G7 CHORD. PLAY THE G7 UNTIL YOU REACH THE C CHORD AGAIN.

— DOWN IN THE VALLEY —

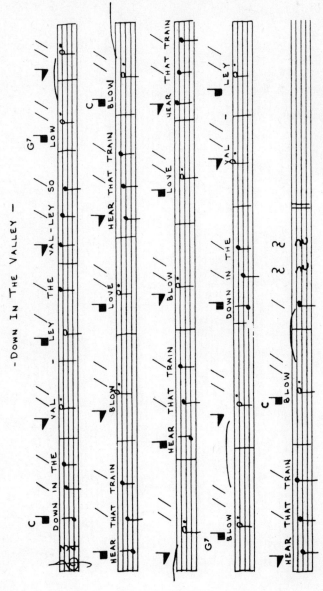

The F Chord

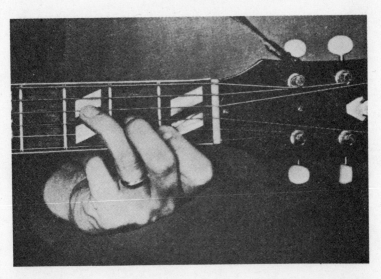

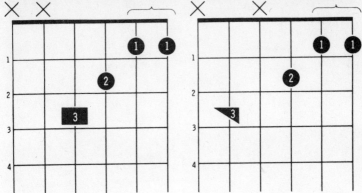

F chord using bass note.   F chord using alternate bass note.

Practice this chord in the same manner as the previous chords.

Practice

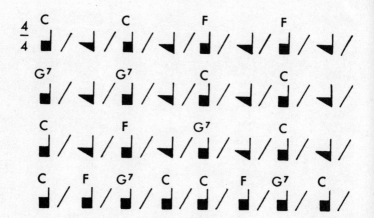

Now let's practice adding the F chord to our repertoire.

On Top of Old Smoky

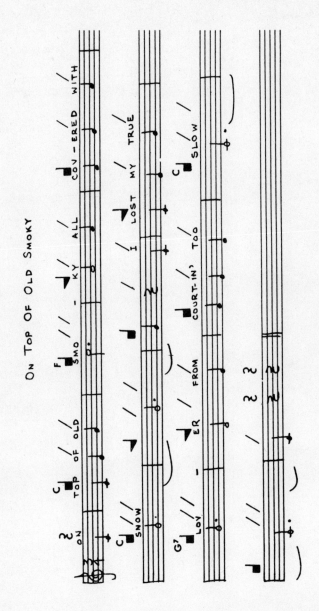

SILENT NIGHT

The D⁷ Chord

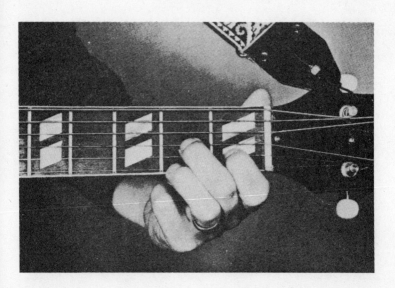

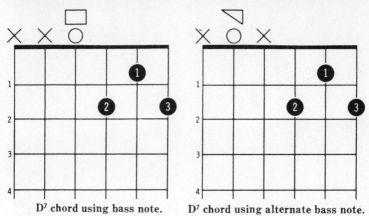

D⁷ chord using bass note.   D⁷ chord using alternate bass note.

Practice this chord in the same manner as the previous chords.

Practice

Let's add still another chord to our library.

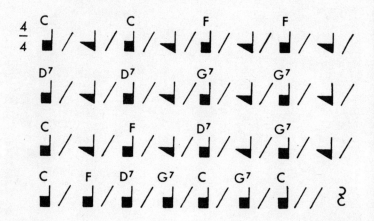

- JINGLE BELLS -

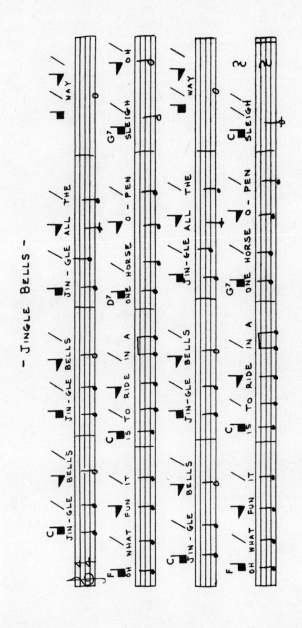

Oh! Susanna

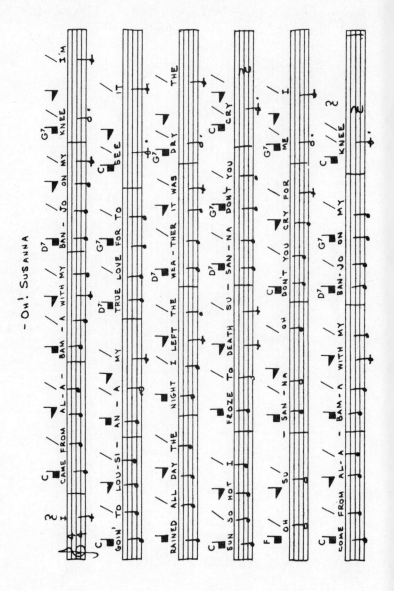

CHORDS IN KEY OF G

The G Chord

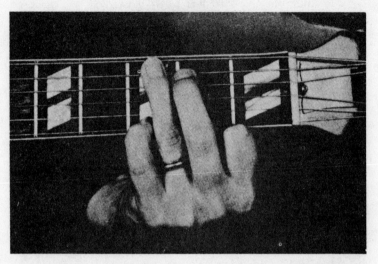

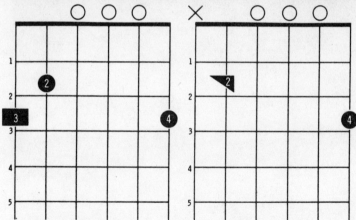

G chord using bass note.   G chord using alternate bass note.

Practice this chord in the same manner.

Practice

Now that the G chord has been mastered, let's practice playing this chord with the D⁷ chord which we learned in "chords in the key of C."

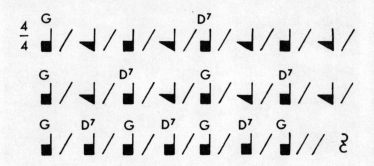

OH, MY DARLING CLEMENTINE

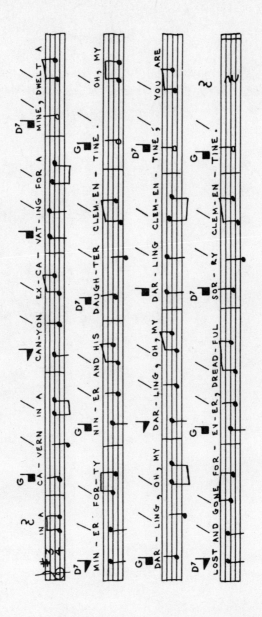

Practice

Let's add another chord to our repertoire in the key of G—our first chord, the C chord. Practice this mixture as shown below:

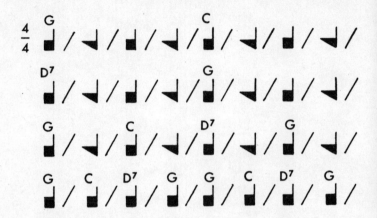

SHE'LL BE COMING ROUND THE MOUNTAIN

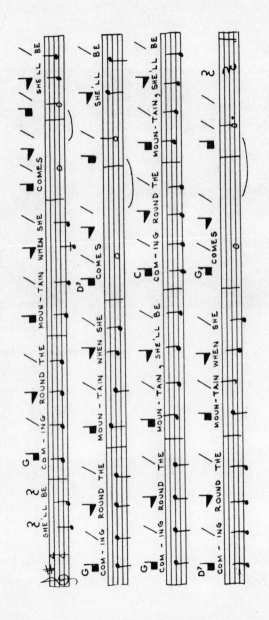

The A⁷ Chord

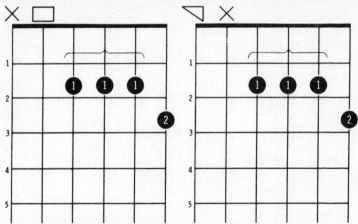

A⁷ chord using bass note. A⁷ chord using alternate bass note.

Practice this chord in the same manner as the previous ones.

Practice

Let's add the A^7 chord to our bag of tricks by practicing as indicated below:

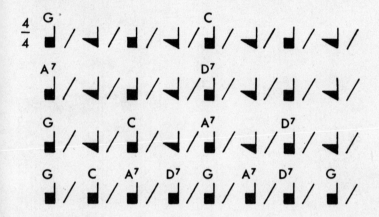

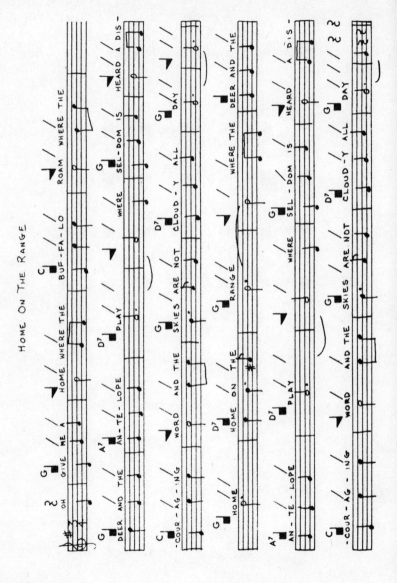

JOLLY OLD ST. NICHOLAS

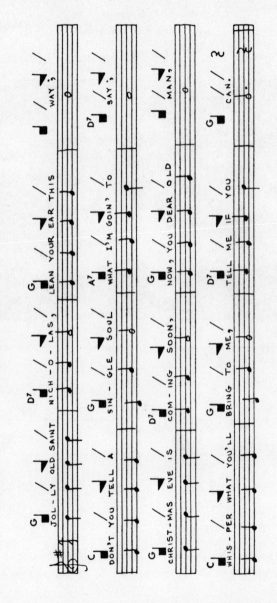

CHORDS IN KEY OF D

The D Chord

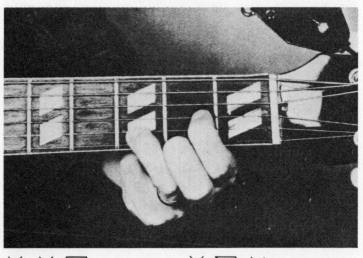

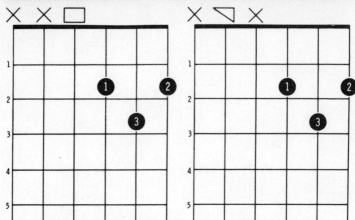

D chord using bass note.   D chord using alternate bass note.

Practice this chord in the same manner as before.

Practice

Let's combine the D chord with the A^7 chord we learned in "chords in key of G." Practice as shown below:

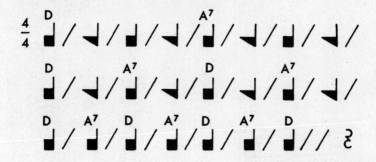

LONG LONG AGO

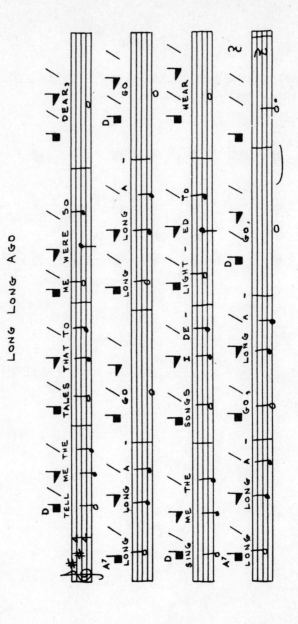

Practice

Our third chord in the key of D is a familiar one—the G chord from "chords in key of G." Let's practice this one as shown below:

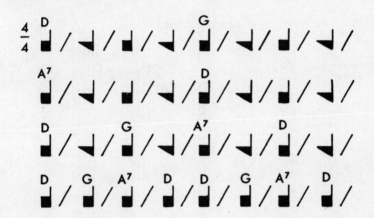

THE MARINES HYMN

47

The E⁷ Chord

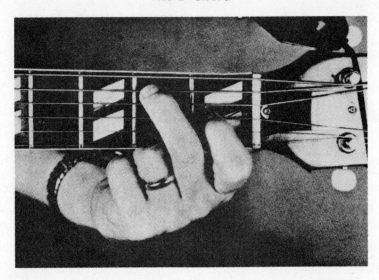

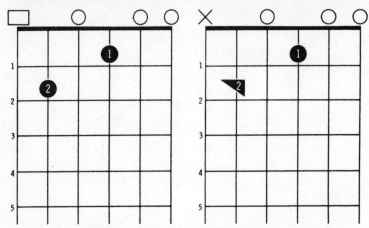

E⁷ chord using bass note.   E⁷ chord using alternate bass note.

Practice this chord until tone becomes clear.

Practice

Let's work the E⁷ chord into our library of chords by practicing as shown below:

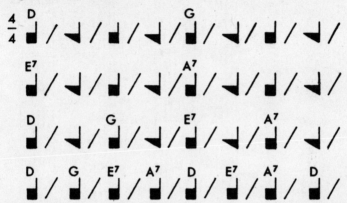

MY BONNIE

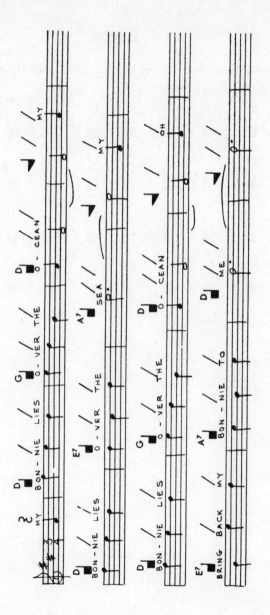

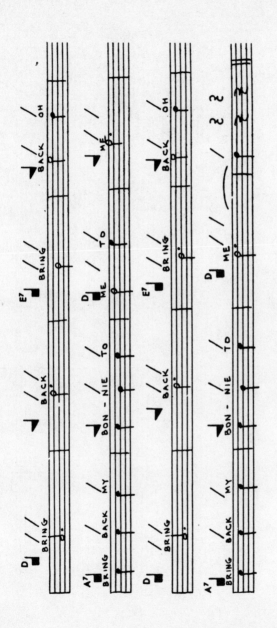

OUR TEAM WILL SHINE

CHORDS IN KEY OF A

The A Chord

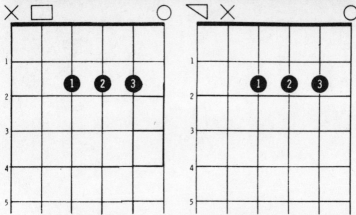

A chord using bass note.   A chord using alternate bass note.

Practice this chord in the same manner as the others.

Practice

Let's pair up the A chord with the E⁷ chord by practicing as shown below:

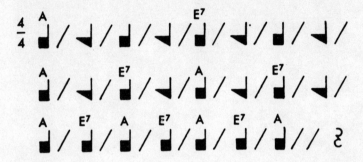

Hand Me Down My Walking Cane

Practice

Our third chord in the key of A is the D chord from "chords in key of D." Let's practice this one as shown below:

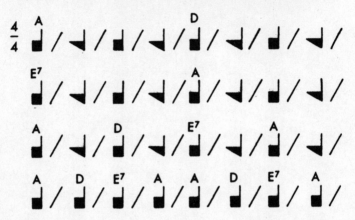

HAPPY BIRTHDAY

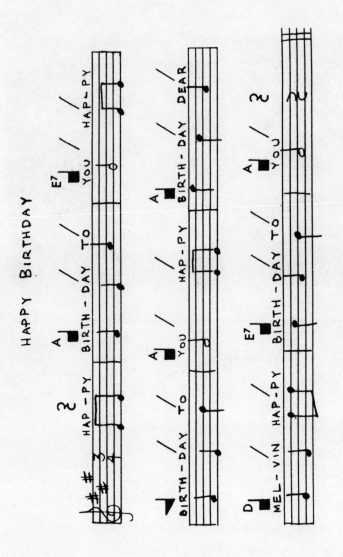

The B⁷ Chord

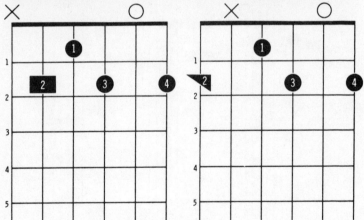

B⁷ chord using bass note.   B⁷ chord using alternate bass note.

Practice this chord until tone is clear.

Practice

Let's add the B^7 chord to our repertoire by practicing as shown below:

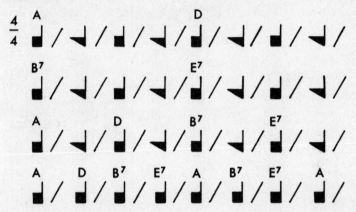

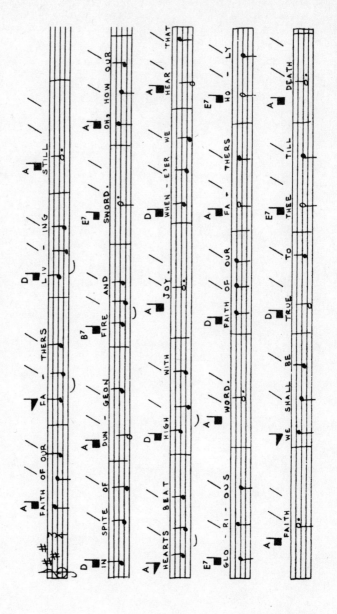

CHORDS IN KEY OF F

The C⁷ Chord

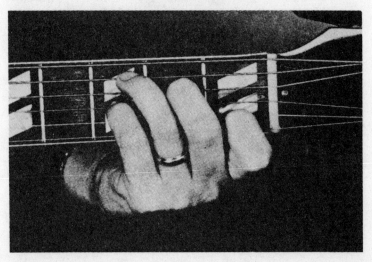

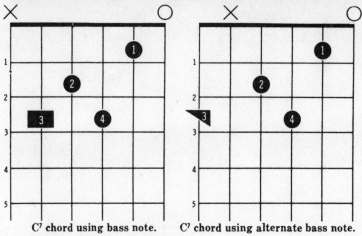

C⁷ chord using bass note.   C⁷ chord using alternate bass note.

Practice until tone becomes clear.

Practice

In the key of F, our tonic or root chord is the F chord which we learned in "chords in key of C." Let's practice this chord and the C^7 chord as shown below:

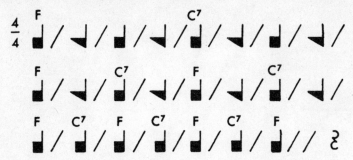

Row, Row, Row Your Boat

The B♭ (B-Flat) Chord

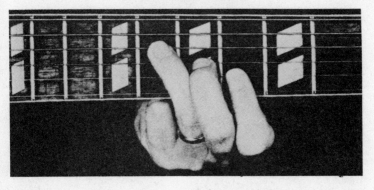

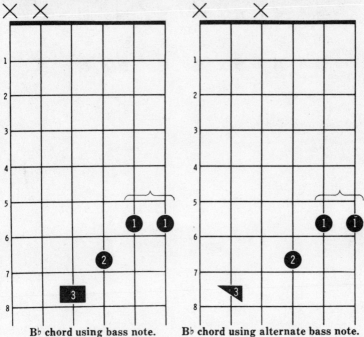

B♭ chord using bass note. B♭ chord using alternate bass note.

Practice until tone becomes clear.

Practice

Let's add the B♭ chord to our library by practicing as shown below:

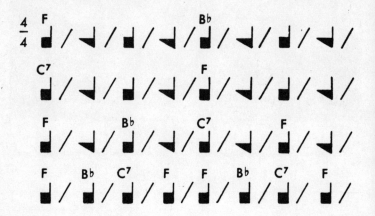

AULD LANG SYNE

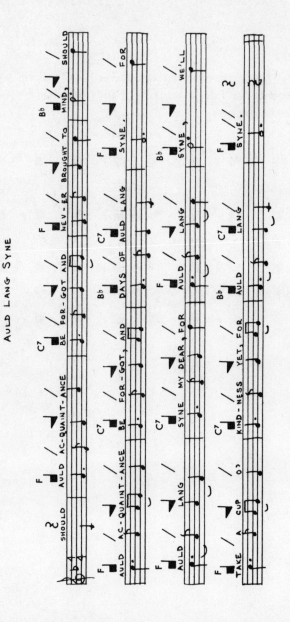

Practice

Our fourth chord in the key of F is the G⁷ chord, which we learned in "chords in key of C." Let's practice this chord as shown below:

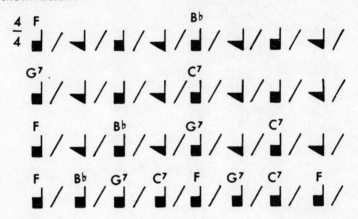

CAMPTOWN RACES

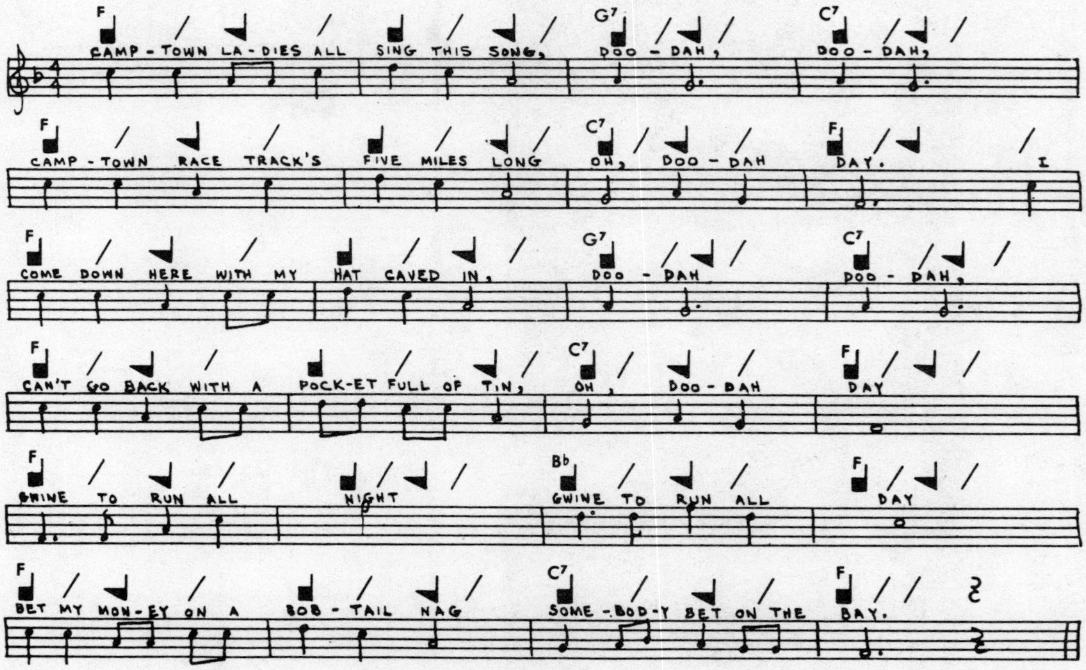

The F⁷ Chord

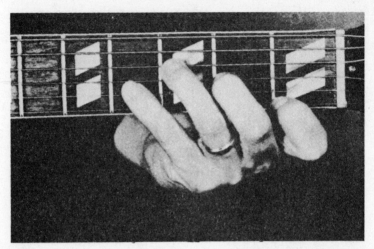

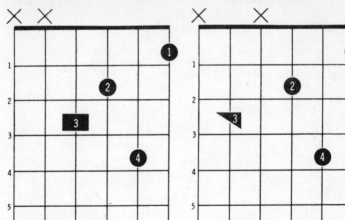

F⁷ chord using bass note.
Practice until tone is clear.

F⁷ chord using alternate bass note.

68

Practice

In the key of B♭, the tonic or root chord is the B♭ chord which we learned in "chords in key of F." Let's practice working the B♭ chord and the F⁷ chord together as shown below:

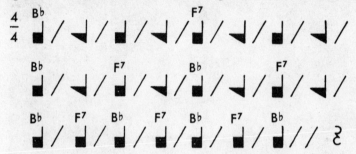

HAIL, HAIL, THE GANG'S ALL HERE

The E♭ Chord

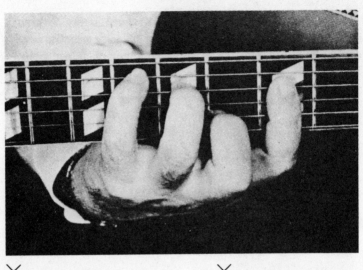

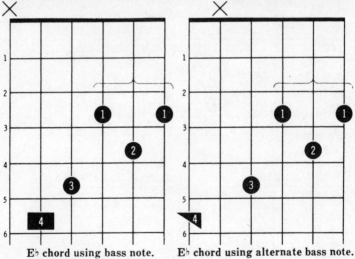

E♭ chord using bass note. Practice until tone is clear.

E♭ chord using alternate bass note.

Practice

Let's work our third chord in by practicing as shown below:

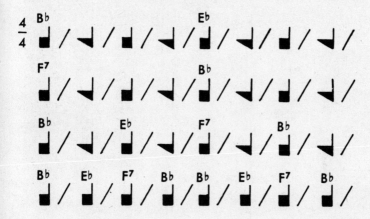

Home Sweet Home

Practice

Our fourth chord in the key of B♭ is the C⁷ chord which we learned in "chords in key of F." Let's add this chord to our B♭ repertoire by practicing as shown below:

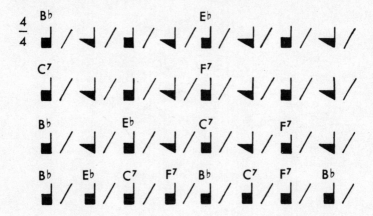

My Wild Irish Rose

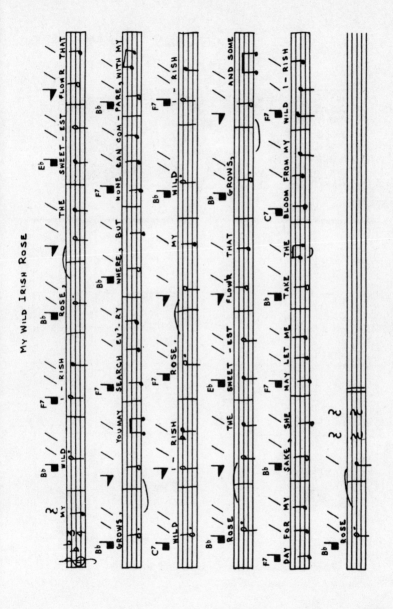

The B♭⁷ Chord

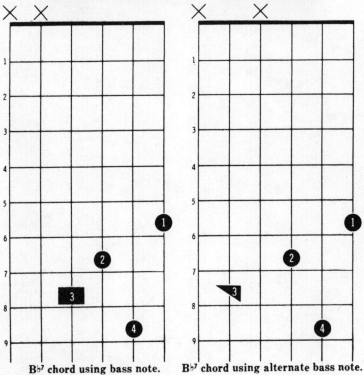

B♭⁷ chord using bass note. Practice until tone is clear.

B♭⁷ chord using alternate bass note.

Practice

In the key of E♭ the tonic or root chord is the E♭ chord which we learned in "chords in key of B♭." Let's practice the E♭ chord and the B♭⁷ chord as shown below:

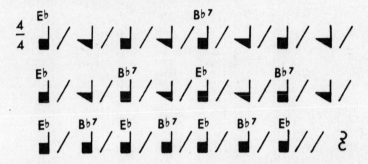

THE GIRL I LEFT BEHIND ME

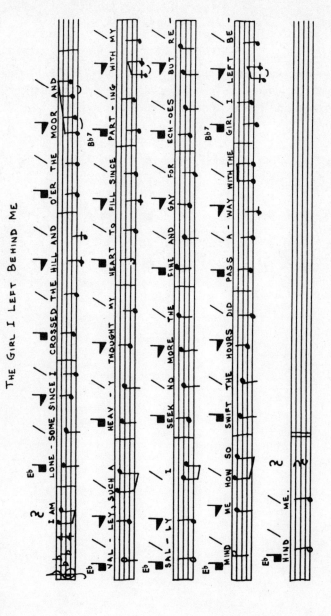

The A♭ Chord

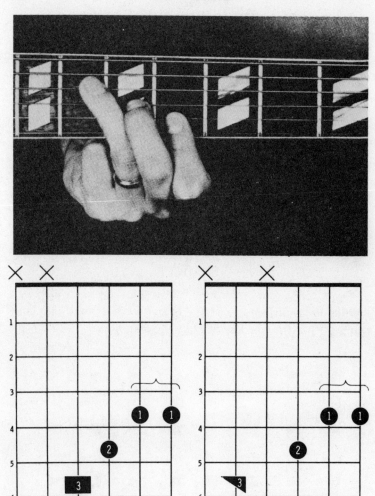

A♭ chord using bass note.　　A♭ chord using alternate bass note.

Practice until tone is clear.

Practice

Let's work the A♭ chord into our repertoire by practicing as shown below:

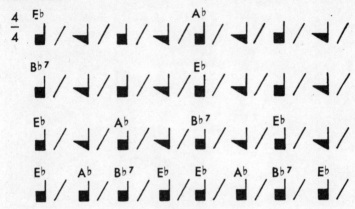

Practice

Our fourth chord in the key of E♭ is the F⁷ chord, which we learned in "chords in key of B♭." Let's work this chord into our string of chords in the key of E♭ by practicing as shown below:

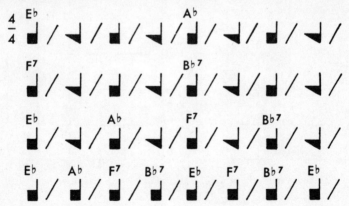

A BICYCLE BUILT FOR TWO

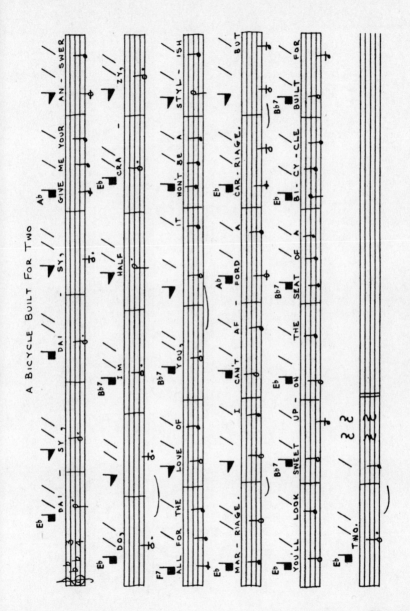

Old Folks At Home

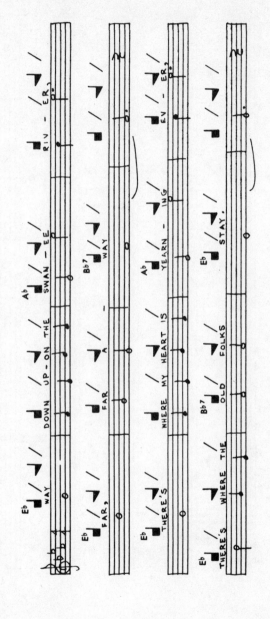

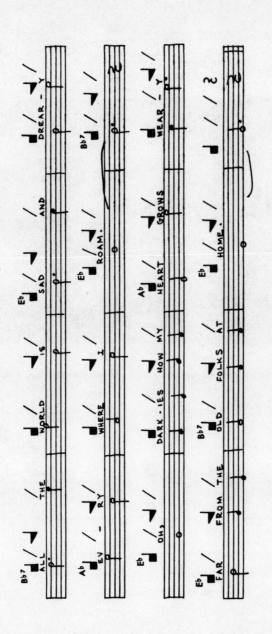

The E^{b7} Chord

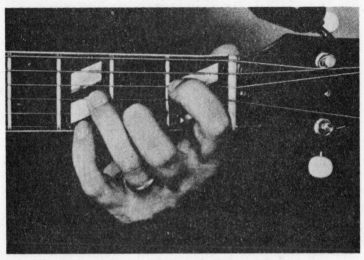

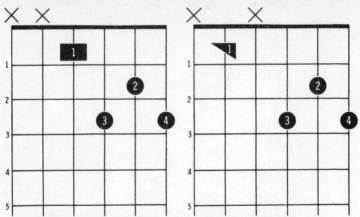

E^{b7} chord using bass note.   E^{b7} chord using alternate bass note.

Practice until tone is clear.

Practice

In the key of A♭, the tonic or root chord is the A♭ chord which we learned in "chords in key of E♭." Let's practice this chord with the E♭⁷ chord as shown below:

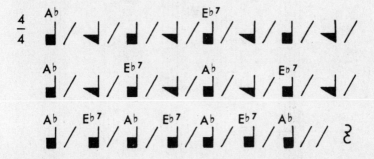

O CHRISTMAS TREE

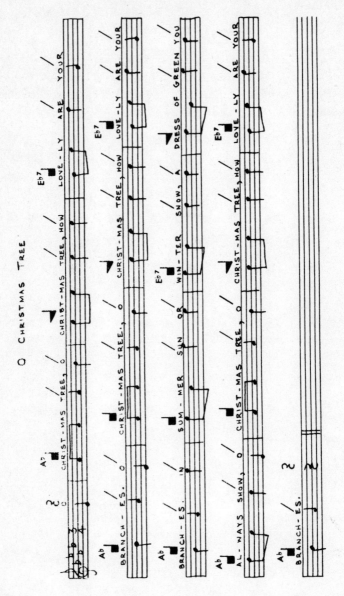

The D♭ Chord

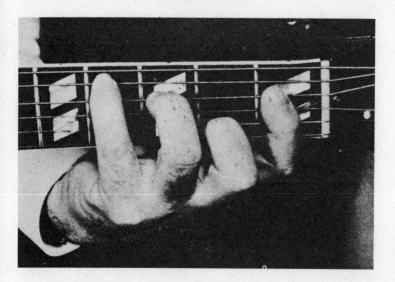

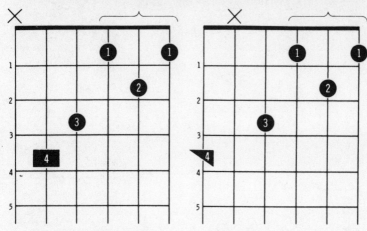

D♭ chord using bass note.
Practice until tone is clear.

D♭ chord using alternate bass note.

Practice

Let's add the D♭ chord to our library by practicing as shown below:

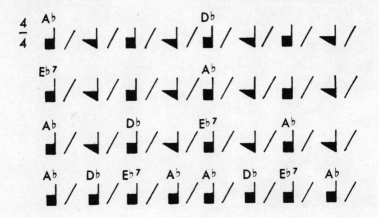

THE OLD GREY MARE

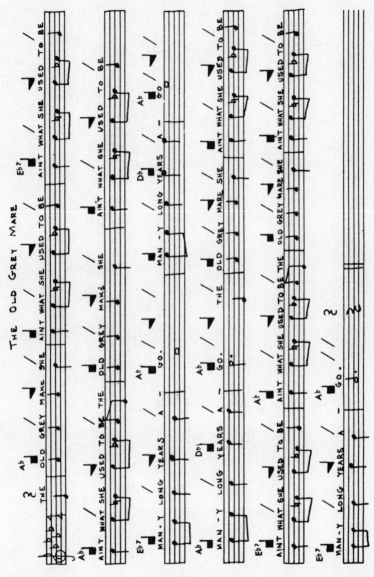

BEAUTIFUL DREAMER

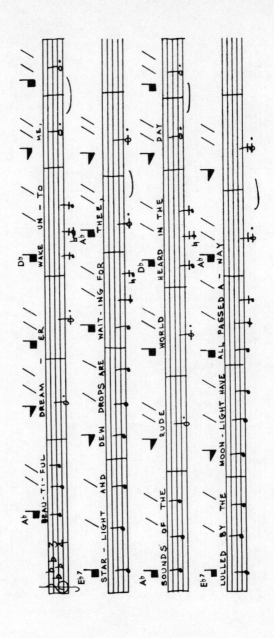

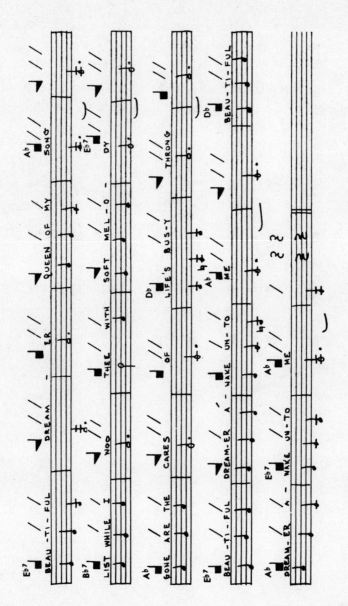

91

Practice

The fourth chord in the key of A♭ is the B♭⁷ chord, which we learned in "chords in key of E♭." Let's work this chord in by practicing as shown below:

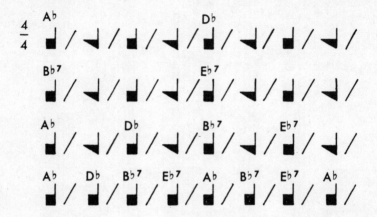

ADDITIONAL PRACTICE SONGS

The two songs in this section were selected as a "final exam" for testing your skill as a guitarist. These songs are slightly more difficult than the other songs; however, you will find that all the chords have been covered in various sections of this book.

I've Been Working On The Railroad

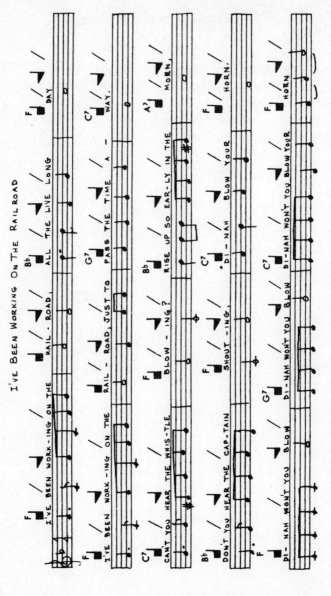

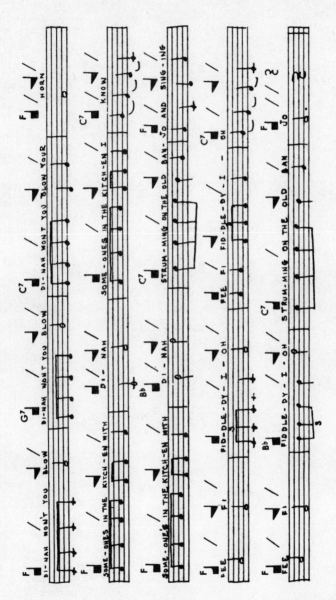

95

You Tell Me Your Dream